I Want More
How to Know When I've Had Enough

Written and Illustrated by
Dagmar Geisler

Translated by
Andrea Jones Berasaluce

Sky Pony Press
New York

Visit our website at www.skyponypress.com.

10 9 8 7 6 5 4 3 2 1

Manufactured in China, November 2019
This product conforms to CPSIA 2008

Library of Congress Cataloging-in-Publication Data is available on file.

Cover design by Elke Kohlmann and Daniel Brount
Cover illustration by Dagmar Geisler

Print ISBN: 978-1-5107-4655-8
Ebook ISBN: 978-1-5107-4666-4

When Do I Really Have Enough?

This question isn't even easy for adults to answer. Small children usually have a good sense of it, though, quickly noticing when something is too much for them. But because there are so many opportunities and, unfortunately, pressures, to go over the natural limit, that inner sense can easily get lost.

Responsible parents will make sure their kid does not stuff him- or herself with an unlimited amount of gummy bears or spend endless hours in front of the TV, just to name two examples of the many things children experience. Nevertheless, it is also important to develop one's own internal feeling for when something has reached its limit. This is especially difficult when it's something of which you actually "can't get enough" of.

When does pleasure stop and when does habituation begin? When someone starts to ask him/herself that, s/he is on a good path; examining this question is a good preventer of addiction. It doesn't matter whether it's gummy bears or French fries, watching television or playing video games . . . the list could go on forever.

But one thing is certain: something's really only fun when a person can say "Now I've had enough."

Dagmar Geisler

I can
never get enough
of most things.

What about you?

My name is Lisa, and I can't get enough gummy bears. I like the yellow and red ones best. But the green ones are also good. And so are the orange ones.

The red ones taste a bit like strawberry, the green ones taste like limes, and the orange ones like oranges.

After the tenth gummy bear, they all taste the same. After the twelfth one, my mouth gets very sticky. And if I eat the entire bag, then . . .

But anyway . . .
I can't get enough gummy bears.
Honest!

My name is Emma, and I think swimming in the bathtub is fantastic. But when I'm swimming, I can tell exactly when I've been under water long enough.

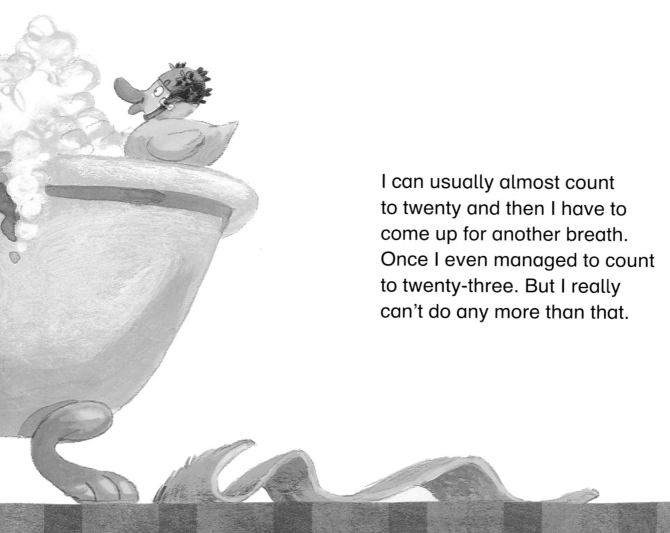

I can usually almost count
to twenty and then I have to
come up for another breath.
Once I even managed to count
to twenty-three. But I really
can't do any more than that.

I'm Tim, and I love Soccer Rabbits. I can't get enough of them. My first one is my favorite rabbit. I got him from Grandma.

She knitted him a long scarf and embroidered his name on his jersey. His name is Fritz, and he's the best striker in the world.

I quickly put together my first soccer team. Fritz is allowed to sleep in my bed and the others have a spot on the shelf above. Suddenly, I had so many rabbits that some had to sit on the dresser and on the windowsill and on my desk. And under the bed and on the carpet and under the chair . . .

Really! I don't have enough Soccer Rabbits. But where did my favorite rabbit go? I can't find him anymore.

Our names are Emilia and Finn, and when we're together, we love to romp around and play. We race up and down hills; we climb and tumble and dash.

But sometimes I get very out of breath. Then I even get cramps in my side.

Sometimes my knees shake. But that doesn't matter.

My name is Lilly, and I have a new jump rope. I like jumping rope. But even more than that, I like everything that glitters.

My hair clips sparkle like dewdrops in a spider's web, and the rhinestones on my T-shirt twinkle like water droplets in our garden fountain.

But I also need a sparkling headband and a glittery bow. And a glittery belt, a glittery backpack, glittery chains, glittery socks, bracelets, and, and, and . . .

But how can I jump rope with all that?

I'm Paul, and I think it's great to hug
and cuddle. I can't get enough.
I love cuddling with Mr. Meow.
He's our cat.

And with Mom . . .

and with Dad.

Grandma always
wants a lot of kisses.

But it's better if I don't tell
Aunt Amelie that I just can't
get enough of hugging.

All right,
where is
he?

I am Marie, and I love watching television so much! My favorite TV show is so funny. My brother thinks so, too. We laugh until we can't breathe. When the show ends, my brother doesn't want to watch any more TV. He'll go out and play.

Now a new show's starting! The other kids are playing outside. I hear them laugh. My brother laughs the loudest. Should I go outside now, too?

Probably . . . but somehow, I feel too weak, and another show is already starting.

The show is on for a while, until after my brother comes back. He is in an awfully good mood and smells like fresh air.

"We had so much fun," he says. "You should've come along. But you just can't get enough TV."

"So what?" I say.

My name is Noah, and I love French fries. I can't get enough of them. I always eat the fries first, no matter what I'm having. And if there are no fries, I sometimes secretly buy myself some. We have a French fry stand right in front of our house.

I like fries best with ketchup. Ketchup is made from tomatoes. Since I like tomatoes so much, Mom said I should plant some myself.

And that's what I did. The tomatoes grow in a pot on the balcony. I have also sown parsley and chives. It took a long time for everything to grow.

I planted everything a while back. Now Mom has made a salad with my own tomatoes and herbs. It looks delicious!

But I can't eat any of it. My stomach is full of French fries. Nothing more can fit inside. Not even the smallest bite.

When have you had enough? And when is it too much? What do you think? Which statement and which smiley face fits with how you're feeling?

All my stuffed animals sleep on my bed. And where should I sleep?

I have to think about gummy bears all the time.

My knees shake.

I don't even realize how good it tastes.

I am very worn-out, but I have no desire to do anything else.

To get into my bed, I need a helicopter.

When running, I feel as light as a bird.

Just right!

Could do a little bit more . . .

A little too little . . .

Too little!

My rabbit has the best spot in my room.

My mouth is very sticky.

I feel a little funny.

This is sooo delicious!

Enough already!

Way too much!

Too much!

I'm actually full, but it tastes so good.

A little too much . . .

We laugh ourselves silly.

Was it really this good . . .?

I feel sick.

Phew! I'm hardly getting any air.

I have been looking forward to this for a long time.

I had French fries the day before yesterday, and yesterday, and again today.

My stomach's so full, not even a little leaf can fit inside.

My Name Is:

My Favorite Thing Is:

I've Had Enough When:

Enough
for today!

Tomorrow's another day.